BLACK MARIA

For Michaelle
& her brilliance
Peace

BLACK MARIA

being the adventures of

DELILAH REDBONE & A.K.A. JONES

POEMS PRODUCED *and* DIRECTED BY

KEVIN YOUNG

ALFRED A. KNOPF, NEW YORK

2005

THIS IS A BORZOI BOOK
PUBLISHED BY ALFRED A. KNOPF

Grateful acknowledgment is made to Curtis Brown Ltd. for permission to reprint "Blues
(for Heidi Anderson)" from *The English Auden*, by W. H. Auden. Copyright © 1937
W. H. Auden. Reprinted by permission of Curtis Brown Ltd.

Library of Congress Cataloging-in-Publication Data
Young, Kevin.
Black Maria : being the adventures of Delilah Redbone and A.K.A. Jones /
Kevin Young— 1st ed.
p.   cm.
ISBN 1-4000-4209-7
1. Man-woman relationships—Poetry.   2. Private investigators—Poetry.   3. City and
town life—Poetry.   4. Young women—Poetry.   I. Title.

PS3575.O798B57 2005
811'.54—dc22
2004048568

Manufactured in the United States of America
Published February 7, 2005
Second Printing, November 2005

for K. J.

I love you as a sheriff searches for a walnut
That will solve a murder case unsolved for years
—KENNETH KOCH

CONTENTS

ONE

HONEYMOON RAIN

I

TWO

STONE ANGELS

45

THREE

LOW NOON

87

FOUR

ALIBI SALOON

131

FIVE

HEMLOCK LANE

181

END TITLES

237

ACKNOWLEDGMENTS

241

BLACK MARIA

{RHYMES WITH PARIAH}

*slang meaning a police wagon
or hearse*

HONEYMOON RAIN

*

If that diamond ring don't shine
Bo Diddley take it to a private eye
—BO DIDDLEY

*Boy meets girl. Girl meets
The City. Nights she sings for her
supper under the stage name Delilah
Redbone; days she avoids the super, and the
casting couch. Boy and girl rendezvous: his place,
her place, a no-tell motel, who can tell. Aliases
and ambushes. Throughout, a hint of a crime, or
at least a world in which everyone's a suspect.
Is she too good (or bad) to be believed?
Can anyone be believed?
Stay tuned.*

THE SET-UP

Snake oil sales
were slow. So I hung

out my shingle on
a shadow.

Desk-drawer liquor

A dead man's loan. Soon
chinless stoolies

slunk & doorjambed—
ratted

that she ain't no
good, that she wears a watch

on both wrists. Too
many midnights.

Evidence mounting like butterflies

Still I made them informants
for phonies, phoned

to hear her breath.
She was faith

enough to believe.
She's a peach. A pistol.

I waived my fee

I left my agency

Came home to rooms ran-
sacked, tossed

by invisible hands.
Hip flask. Blackjacked.

Swig,
mickey slip, slug.

I woke doubled & crossed

Drug, ferried
through whisky alleys

Bruisers, suicide doors

The crooked chief interrogated
me about her body

She's no more mine, no eye
witness, nor alibi

No one will attest she ever
did exist.

I was her autumn guy

By the wharf was left
waterlogged & wise

My dogs dead
tired, I humped it

home, humming gumshoe blues.

THE CHASE

I didn't have a rat's chance.
Soon as she walked in in

That skin of hers
violins began. You could half hear

The typewriters jabber
as she jawed on: *fee, find, me,*

poor, please.
Shadows & smiles, she was.

Strong scent of before-rain

Her pinstripe two-lane
legs, her blackmail menthol.

She had all the negatives

Hidden safe
& would not reveal the place.

Before you could say
denouement, I was on her case—

Slant hat, broad
back, my entrenched coat

Of fog. Fleabags,
neon blinds undrawn—

The foreshadows fell on her face.

All night I tailed, staked
the joint. Found

Her with the butler
playing patty-cake.

Baker's man. She nurse
him like beer

Till dawn. Doozy.
Was from her woozy,

My eyes wet.
Binocular mist.

I took two to the chest

Was all
rain, her blurring face

Her snuffed, stubbed-out
lipstuck cigarette.

SPEAKEASY

The band vamped,
sunlight leaving—sequined,

Delilah Redbone swung
her hardships & sang—

Sporting my lucky
hundred-proof cologne

I listened hard at the bar
as the houselights dimmed—

Rich widows passed matches
with messages in the flaps

Weary husbands with ring-
worn hands sweated

Like their drinks, getting up
the nerve to ask.

I tossed a few back

The band cranked, sharp,
trumpet neath a hat—

Glasses & dance
cards empty, ladies winked

For a light so often
—*Say, mister*—

You'd think you were
the election-year mayor

Handing out favors.
Every joe here

Named John or Jack
or Hey You or Doe—

My answer, mostly, *No.*

Another round & the band
blew its medley midnight

Husbands hugged
their mistresses tighter

And she scat till the moon
caught itself

In the trees like a balloon
let go by a child, crying,

At the county fair.
My saltwater

Shotglass. My flask

Full of lighter fluid.
The piano boogied twilight

She sang & swooned & the sun
started up

An argument with what was left
of the dark—

The swingshift stumbled out

The graveyard drug in thirsty
& worse. Delilah sang on

About hearts that break like high-note
glass—or jaws—

That break more than men
in the mob-run union.

The band beat louder
passing a hat, damping

Foreheads with *uh-huh*s
& handkerchiefs

While Miss Redbone sang:

Lord, I'm afraid
Whoa, so afraid

I done married Mud
& took on his name.

THE HUNCH

She wore red like a razor—
cut quite a figure

standing there, her
slender danger

dividing day
from night, there

from here. Where
I hoped to be is near

her & her
fragrant, flammable hair—

words like *always*
entering my mouth

that once only gargled doubt.

You see, I been used
before like a car . . .

Between us
this sweating, a grandfather

clock's steady tick, soundtrack
of saxophones sighing.

It's been too long—
a whole week

since love burned
me like rye. I had begun

to see the glass
as never empty

& that scared me.

She fills me
like the lake

fills a canoe—
no rescue—& to swim

I never learned how.

THE CHANTEUSE

I was born down the road
where there ain't no

roads—no pictures
no producers neither—

I danced to the radio

when it wasn't singing Sunday,
auditioned for the locusts

and mocking-
birds, the chickens

who never hollered *Cut.*

Soon I knew I had to see
my screen fill with sun

and grabbed me a morning train
to pull my way here

where stars paparazzi the ground.

Now, the five stories
to my flat keep me fit—

that, and a hot plate, a cold
can of beans whose jagged lid

opens your hand
as if charity. Giving

blood. Here
the couch has a caste

all its own—the can-can
line each night grows broader

the kicks higher

but still sounds better
than the soup line.

Soon the world might want
to hear a country girl sing

bout her last good thing—

Said soon the world might
want itself to hear

this country girl sing bout
her last good thing—

Earn my hand a green-gold ring.

Till then the nights fill
with what I know

must be stars beyond
flickering streetlights, the haze—

I've learned that even after
it sets, the smallest sun can stay,

your eyelids stain—

if you stare straight
at it, a camera, don't look away.

THE PROPS

Late afternoon light drenched
in rotgut

Gun belonging to no one

The poor patsy
The sassy secretary

The shabby best
friend in seersucker

Shoulder pads
and highwaist pants

Pinstripe patter

The singer at the local
color watering hole

What a looker!

Powder-room visit to put
on her face

Lowered shade
Conk and pomade

The sky
a dark sedan strafed

By a tommy gun

A manhattan
An old fashioned

Stars bulletholes that let
in light

The pillowed pistol
drawn like a drink, shot

My neck-
tie caught

Up in the machine of night

DRESS CODE

Start with a kind
of happiness

only serious
drink can cure.

*

      Black suit.
      White socks.

*

Trust no one, especially
yourself

not to mention men
wearing belts

& suspenders both.

*

Roscoe?   check.

Blank rounds
for effect

Sunglasses that ensure
dark clouds

Jacket of flak   check.

Spectacles testicles
wallet & keys

check
check check.

*

You'll need
a middle name—

mine's Danger.
Or, Minor Displeasure.

＊

I carry 6 false IDs
that double as skeleton keys—

3 salesmen
(vacuum, burial, bible)

1 inspector
of health

1 detective (homicide)
1 clergy (denomination, you decide).

＊

Wingtips.
Four-in-hand.

Handkerchiefs touch-up
foreheads like photographs.

＊

Pockets full of voices
I've recorded.

＊

Reminder: take

a thick French accent
a fake mustache

tortoiseshell glasses (faux)
& a beaver hat

just in case
you have to make a break

or impersonate.

*

Carry you
a stogie

cheap as a mortician's suit,
that stink . . .

*

but don't smoke.
You'll need

keep your kisser fresh
for lips

& lies.

*

Day or night
the shadow below my nose,

my sundial face, stays
5 o'clock.

*

Without warning be prepared

to get out of Dodge
& flee the swampy city

Learn to live out a suitcase
or as one—you are

{20}

a chifforobe with wheels
wearing everything you need.

*

How to pack in the dark:
a book

of matches from the corner dive
your only light

No goodbyes

And above you the moon
a bruise or its aspirin—

a shiner even dark
glasses can't hide.

{21}

PREMIERE

The starlets
    were shining. Brandy,

Hot Toddy, Shirley
    Temples—all

lined up the bar & down
    the hatch.

Tired of his tireless
    talk, his so

on, his jargon
    which jarred me asleep—

I tossed on my leopard-
    collar coat

muffler, stole, minx

& took a hike.
    Climbed my fifth-floor

walk-up, the tub
    a kitchen table

the radio a neighbor's
    which gossiped the paper

walls. Was all

I wanted—a month
    that didn't mean rent,

a rent that wasn't
    already spent

hiding from the super.

Fool me fell
    for that underworld

investigator's flowers

when I should've stayed
    minding Mama's garden.

Now no groceries, no mice
    to keep me company,

no men ringing
    except ham-handed him—

the operator who patches
    my make-do man through

calls me *Hon* & gives out
    advice for free: *Lady,*

he ain't worth it. I never
    take her word,

just the El toward
    his place—the street

rising to meet
    me—the grates grabbing

at my heels—steam
    escaping heavenward

from some unseen
    spring beneath.

RENDEZVOUS

Her negligent negligee
Her good nightie

Her bare teddy
Fussy bustier

And trusty bikini—

She hate even
that word, *panty*—

The city a dragnet
My detente haircut

My citizen's arrest
Moonshine room all muss—

Lady, you make me lose
myself & cuss—

Three-inch cuffs
My belt

Snaking the no-tell floor
booked by the hour

Sock garters

My boxers
a knockout—

Her noble camisole
flees her body, wholly

And she is above me
floating, dyed

Hair caught
in stars & aureoles—

Lingering cigarette light

Bolted-down seascape art
Persistent static radio

My growing, gibbous heart—

THE HUSH

For those few nights
we were husband & wife—

Mister & Missus
Smith was the name

we registered under,
laughing ourselves low.

Let the busybody bellboy stare.

I didn't care—
all night Mister Smith's arms

were long enough
to reach round me

& touch—to lift up
& threshold me

to the buckling bed.
There was no one else

in the joint,
it felt, just us knocking

the paint-by-numbers
pictures aslant, ordering up

whatever food they had—
some paper-bag gin—

I didn't care—
pulled the pins

like a grenade's
from my hair

& let the flowers
wilt behind my ear.

Let whisky weather
my throat

& still tomorrow I'll sing—

Let the weather
spill its liquor

wherever it wants.
I'll sink

to that. Who cares
what the world went on

doing—those few nights
& lies & sneaky-pete wine

that made us newlyweds
made sense—

Those nights the only rings

we owned
were those we left behind

from drinks sweating
on the warped wood,

the wobbly vanity, all
over everything.

STILLS

With her, guilty
was my only plea.

*

When we kiss, her leg kicks
up like a chorus line!

*

The next day what awaits: flat fizz,
an ache cured only by bitters.

*

Two eggs,
over queasy.

*

Chew fat. Spit
blood. Gargle peroxide. Repeat.

*

She's pro
bono, a quid pro.

*

I've given, like gin,
her up, again.

*

Even my shadow
has me followed.

THE INGENUE

Upstairs, that sickle moon
slays me—mows me

On down. Takes
me home, where

Mama bent till dark
tending rows to send

Me to school—
instead I said I wanted

To head on & hitch
that 4:20, strike it

Big. Mama didn't try
stopping me with my

Hard head—said
Fine, child, go head on

Just beware the boys
And don't listen

To them blues

Said beware
the mens and don't listen

To no blues

And tuck this here money
into your shoes.

I pinned it instead
in the girdle she made

Me wear—
Who knew there

Was the first place
anyone'd get to?

＊

At rest stops, slicksters
& shysters tried all angles

to get me to flash my whites:
What's shakin, Red?

the vets said, but I didn't dare.
Ahead I'd stare,

cardboard luggage
locked by my ankles.

*Hincty, 'loof,
dicty,* they called me

but what did I care?
I walk with my chin

in the air.

＊

Course, that was before
I arrived in this neon town

& began to get turned down
twice a day like a rich man's bed

by studio heads. Even then,

whenever I walk out the office
in my one good dress—

a night-blue shift
covered in polka dots

like stars—
my hips turn them spots

to comets, tailing by,

that if you're lucky
may visit more than once

a lifetime. For that
men wait, watch

my waist constellate

through glasses thick or
opera or spy or reading—

they waste their little wishes.

STILLS

When we met, her first request:
Got a light?

*

I only had dark
so gave her that instead.

*

Once I looked rose-colored;
now I see only red.

*

Her cigarettes burn
along just one side:

*

Someone else thunk
bout her all the time.

*

On my door I hung a sign:
GONE WISHING. BACK IN 5.

*

Ashtray full of butts
& maybes.

*

The echo of her heels down the hall
to me means reveille.

THE OFFICE

His diploma from Hard
Knocks College

Hung there askew.
His cologne—

Smelling salts—filled
the messy room.

The name on his lambskin
scrawled in Pig Latin.

No heat—
except what steamed

Between us—
his breath blew rings.

My uncomfortable
underthings.

My eyebrows
plucked apostrophes

Making him mine.

Like a heart my feet ached
after climbing the steep stairs

In skyscraper heels
to his semi-suite. His assistant—

Miss McGuffin—
buzzed me in.

I talked circles
round him, his bachelor's

Degree in bourbon
& silence stood

Him well. What
I gave him: The Soft

Sell. The Hard Luck Tale.
The Runaround. The Quick

Take. The Hayseed.
The Switcheroo. The Second Guess

& Third Degree.

The lights flickered
on & off, the street.

He lit another stogie—

I never did mind his cigars,
their peat, though most thought

They reeked
of horses in the field.

Honestly, that hint
of home is what

I'd missed—
He was biscuits

& figs, was sweet
potato pie cooling

On the sill. Suddenly,
the somewhere I had to be

Went away—
I even wanted to reveal

My real name.

Instead, sweated
in the cold.

Like an old lady
at the matinee

I popped a noisy mint
as if that would help me

Not breathe mist—

My threadbare fur.
My secondhand

Story. Still, for me
he'll fall like Jericho's walls—

You see, he still believed
in something—

Even if it was me,
his losing big-bet team.

I'll quick cure
him of that.

I tried telling him
my maiden name was Trouble

But even that was too much
like a touch

Of perfume behind my ear,
my neck & knees,

That he needed to get near
Just to be sure . . .

His hair dark
as a sparrow's tail

That soon I'll sprinkle
with salt & grey

So he'll never fly away.

THE SUBPLOT

Figures. Her chloroform perfume
flushing my face, my nose

Open for her all night
like a diner. Flickering

Overhead lights.

Woke blind as a date, folded,
fighting my binds

My mouth tied, trying
to not say

What I want. Never

Noticed before: Her mad-
scientist stare

Her quarrelsome hair
Her Igor paramour

And hidden lair.
How did I get here

Among blips & blinks
& tubes useless?

Yesterday in her arms
safe as a police frequency

Band no one could touch

Today I'm just a potion brought
to a boil, green

& smoking
as if after—or before—

Last night lightning
twice roused me while strapped

Down on a slab
in her fabulous lab—

Today I am death's dormouse
gnawing my way out

Of this trap
of cheese, this bit part.

Once she exposes
her plot predictable

I will all evil foil

Finding the serum, the sauce,
what antidote will save

Me—the world—to live
another & love, down ocean

After ocean of

THE ALIAS

Bruised like gin
stirred too quick

Ruining the tonic

I stumbled home
put on a steak eye-patch

& fixed me another drink
hoping this one would take

The way she never did.
On the rocks

& stiff. Alls
I got left—

A key to a safe
deposit that's empty

& one lousey alias—
S.O.S. Mallone.

(My real name's
A.K.A. Jones.

Leastwise
that's what I been told.)

Hey buddy, welcome home—

Murphy bed like a booby
trap, springs shot

My mattress thin as the bills
I once stuffed it with.

I drink a lot
about my thinking problem—

Nightcap,
noontime nip—

She my unquit habit.

This roof with more
leaks than I

Could ever fix, buckets
of rusty rainwater I bend

Low to drink. Brimming over,

My good eye watched
all night the storm

Drown the street in worms

THE SUSPECTS

Threatening rain

The boozy,
overdressed dame

with a voice to match

The unbent bootblack

The one-armed pickpocket
with a nose

for the horses
Informant shot in his tracks

Pullman porter
with a chemistry degree

A well-minxed martini

Last of the light

Too much shadow
around the eyes

Newshound nosing round
the place

Throat cut
like a phone line

An assignation
The asinine accomplice

Here comes the bribe

The day player
who flubs his line

The prizefighter's
blackmail fall

Mousey majorette
at the used bookstore

who unbuttons her hair
& lets down her blouse

Misplaced lightning

Face full of smoke

Character actor
whose accent changes more

than a leading lady's wardrobe

The once-over
The okie-doke

The moon a thumb-
print pressed

in the black police book
kept by the night

Put your hands
where I can see em

Cryptic telegram

Slow cigar ash

And Death, the well-
dressed doorman,

his pockets stuffed with cash.

STONE ANGELS

*

I am a hoodlum, you are a hoodlum, we and all of us
are a world of hoodlums—maybe so.
—CARL SANDBURG

VOICEOVER

(reel two)

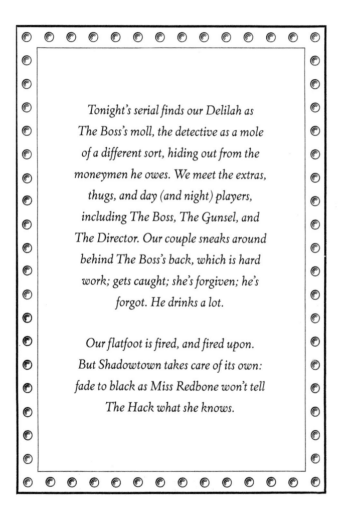

Tonight's serial finds our Delilah as
The Boss's moll, the detective as a mole
of a different sort, hiding out from the
moneymen he owes. We meet the extras,
thugs, and day (and night) players,
including The Boss, The Gunsel, and
The Director. Our couple sneaks around
behind The Boss's back, which is hard
work; gets caught; she's forgiven; he's
forgot. He drinks a lot.

Our flatfoot is fired, and fired upon.
But Shadowtown takes care of its own:
fade to black as Miss Redbone won't tell
The Hack what she knows.

THE BOSS

Even his walking,
stick was crooked.

He didn't need it,
or me, he'd say—let me

know he kept us both
for show. His hands

clean as a cop's whistle,
nails filed

to toothpicks. Slick—
he taught me

to kiss, & silence,
how to tell tons

just from the eyes.
His were ice

picks, raised,

or icebergs tearing
into the berth

of some *Titanic*.
Watch em sink.

He was never in between—
either gargantuan

or thin
as a lie. He sharpened

knives on other men's spines.
He hated losing

even a dime, would bet
the farm, then steal

from the till. Weed em
& reap.

He treated me
like his money—took me

out only
when he needed something

& fast.
Even his toupee—

imported, real
human hair—was one-sided

& levitated
above his head like a lightbulb

burned dim.
No wonder when

that detective stumbled in—

smelling of catharsis
& cheap *ennui,*

begging to be
given an extra week

with his knees—
I wanted him like nobody's

business. His
blown kiss.

Never laundered
like money, that dick's suit

stayed rumpled like the pages
of a paperback dropped

in the tub, drowned, the end
you read first to find out

whodunit, never
mind why.

THE RACES

I regret the day

she ever darkened
my doorway, scented

of rosemary & *eau
de bourbon*—

Now it's all over
town how she treated me

like some Christmas toy
come New Year's—ignored

or broken, left in
a corner. Donate me

to charity, or least
my body—though science can't use me

the way she did, cutting
my insides on out.

Should have followed
my gut & not

this stammering heart. It
sent me straight

to the track, cursing
my luck—there, Ghost

of a Chance beat out
Farmer's Dance

by a nose & I saw
my escape-hatch cash

turn to ash.
And on the last stretch, too—

I knew soon I'd be took
out back, leg broke,

& shot—my shoes
boiled to glue—

while she sat in the stands
beneath a bright hat, using

hundreds, once mine,
like a church fan—cooling

both her faces.

THE RUSE

Have I got one for you.
Might have expected such

from Trixie or even
sullen Sadie

upsweep Mary
or loyal Magdalena

with the lie-gap grin

but never from she
who sailed the days

with me in tow.
You never know.

*

She knew her way
round my ink blotter

like a Rorschach, my office
all clutter ever since

that first day in the Downluck Diner

when I saw her
over the regulars

& a slice of Eve's famous
apple pie with melted cheese.

Was drawn to her
parfum dangereuse

like a barfly to cigarette paper.
Her nails long

as a coffin's—
Her peeling polish.

*

She had me signing
away everything

I kept no carbons

I forget even what
our code word was

Only soon everything stood
for something else:

Sure meant never
Eight meant eleven

o'clock if at all
My girlfriend Jody

was whomever
else she called Daddy.

By the way, *Dame*

still meant lady,
broad, miss

who werewolfs me like this

Who up & quit me
like the Midsummer Motor Company.

*

Filled up
with sorry

& single-man scotch

I fumed, stalling out
my jalopy across the tracks

—Forgive my French—

I gunned & gave it
some juice

& ended out killing
the whole bottle.

　　　※

Train whistle, screech, side-
swipe, dissolve . . .

　　　※

Fade in, interior: St. Jude
Infirmary.

I wake flusterated,

outfoxed, shortsheeted
& -sighted.

Food pre-chewed

Full-body cast

I don't even know where
to begin to point

when Doc Goodnight asks
Do it hurt?

THE GUNSEL

Armed like his teeth

Nervous as a thief
at the cop convention

A ballerina before
a buffet

He laughed loud
& overlong

At The Boss Man's jokes—
again, the one about the senator

& the nun. Something
about bad habits . . .

His were spitting
& cursing, a fondness

For the edge of things:
towns, skirts, a drizzle

That seemed to fall
only when least fitting,

Or most. Love scenes
& holdup schemes.

          *

He smoked for show,
kept the top dog's highball

Full a ice like
chewed glass. Kept his own

Brass knuckles polished
by breath & sweat—

His walk favored his left

Ever since that incident
with the mayor's wife

& two full flights
had gimped his right.

＊

Squirrelly, he kept quiet & his eye
on me always—sideways

He watched me that summer
I made the swimming pool

My bedside table, the moon
my chaperone—

Was paid to see if my heart hurried
when I saw that detective

Slur & slink his way into the room.

But toss a few smiles, maybe a strut,
his way & that guard

Dog would turn lap dog—
he'd fetch & beg but never stay—

Knew neither would I.

＊

The day I did split
my beau The Boss was out

Cold, KO'd by drink

Wearing my stocking
as a cap & snoring

The symphony in Z.

I stuffed my hatbox
full, left only perfume

Littering the room.
Despite the echo

between his ears, that flunky
heard me, the stairs creaky

As his bones. Don't know why

That hired fist let me
walk, a head start, while

He & the night watched—

Just spat his shoes
till they shone

Like exclamation points,
said *See youse*

& wished me dead
& luck.

THE RUSHES

I had everything arranged

I bought orchids
her favorite shade

Received this hot tip
from a dice-eyed snitch

Gave him something bottled up
in exchange

For her real name

This stoolie told me all
odds stacked against me

The 10-to-1 bookie

Who called her cookie,
trouble, doll

The gangster moll

Had sworn me legs
broke to match my heart.

I laughed & ordered up
another tall

Bottle of tales. Deal
me in. Suicide kings.

*

Planned she & I would meet
where the dead sleep, pretending

No one there knew me—

Beneath the morgue moon,
blue light tugging at seas

One day, I thought, that
will be me

In the godawful ground—

Our kisses cemeteries

The suicides coughing
in their restless deep

The moon autopsied
to find out if it waned

From natural causes.
Bulletproof hearses.

＊

Soon my frame grew
hazy, swayed

As if memory
is not this etched thing

A useless machine

I dreamt the sleep that sews
the eyes up

Loan-shark chums
bobbing shallow water

Recall what happened last
time we held—

How like a trapped
parrot she talked

How soon she sang

*

I snapped back to see
her hushed beside me

Soft-focus frame fading

The fedoraed darkness moving—

Our arms open
as fire, we embraced

While bullets ricocheted
off stone angels

Worn down by weather
& winnowed by tears

Of red-clad widows
in crocodile heels

Who visit just one hour a year.

EARLY SHOW

Here even the darkness
is watered down—

Shades drawn
won't keep out dawn,

Won't bring me sleep
or us any closer—

The gap in our pushed-together
twin beds grows wider.

Regret a green thing
all morning I been

Watering—not that
it needs it—

Even untended my mind
weed-filled, wild.

Nothing wakes him—
not the trucks' hum

Backing up, not the woman
who knocks loud, trading

The hotel's ghostly towels
but letting the sheets

Stay unchanged.

Lunchtime,
the adultery hour—

The flophouse fills
with couples telling

Work they need
an extra hour

For the doctor—
you can hear them in the hall

Practicing coughs
& examining each

Other's tonsils. *Ah*—

If despair had a sound
it would be: DO NOT DISTURB.

If despair has a sound
it's the muffled, raised

Voices of the pair next door
who've lived here

In One-Star Manor forever
yet still pay by the week

—Love's an iffy lease—

Or worse may be
the sharp silence

That follows every fight.
While the secretaries

& file clerks & junior
execs undress—

Trade their shorthand kisses—

I run what HOT
is left (though hard

To know, marked COLD)
till I steam the mirrors

Like car windows
in a prom's parking lot

& I can't see myself.

Despair,
I know, is the ham radio

On low, crackling
like rain & announcing

Today's game
has been called—a first—

On account of too much sun.

STILLS

We undress shy
as a gun.

*

The mailman's son, I am
nor snow, nor night, nor gloom.

*

Her eyelashes long
& false as an alarm.

*

He say, she say,
foreplay, amscray.

*

Her cocktail dress pours
over my bare floor.

*

Her feather boa
hissing *yes.*

*

Without her I am incomplete—
prehensible, licit, couth.

*

Wisdom this tooth
aching I want removed.

SATURDAY MATINEE

The organ-grinder monkey grinds
The ambulance's endless whine

I can't stop for either—
no time. I'm on my way

To meet he who calls me
blame, or a crime—tonic

With two limes—
who thinks I am something else

To sleuth and file
UNSOLVED.

I pay him no mind.
My reply: to laugh

And survive.
See, Detective, where I live

No one's thin
as a film strip

And I get me good advice:
Now, 'Lilah, my girls say,

*Don't you worry
yourself over no man.*

And,
Cold heart, warm hands.

But these days no flame
lights the pilot below the range

These days the radiator knocks
so quiet a gal wants

Someone strong to unlock
the door, keep her dogs hot.

Outside the ambulances
whir by, sirens

Drowning our fuss—my cries—

All night the radiator knocks
so quiet a gal wants

Someone strong to pick
her lock, his hands

Delicate and hot.

THE FRAME

Wearing silver like a screen

She stood, leaned,
purred words I waited

Wanted an audience to hear.
Throat-hearted,

I wore gin
as if it was cologne

Or cotton. Seersucker.

She spoke & her tongue forked
through that glorious gap

In her fronts.
She boohooed & cooed

I folded

& refolded my kerchief
like a bad hand

I'd been dealt.
Ace, spade, one-eyed

Jack, I peeked out the blinds
at the streetlight silhouette

Her inevitable tail.

Blinded by those falsehooded eyes
her bright, boomerang smile

I begged to choose her—

How could I know she wore
a wire under

Her bulletproof bra?

She tapped me good,
told anyone

Who would listen
my business—the 36,

24, 38 that clicked open
my fireproof safe.

Trouble's shot me down again

To the quarter where
the light stays scarlet

Where the blues share
your by-the-hour bed

Where only green
speaks, cares, how

& who the hell you been.

THE HOOCH

Her eyes whisky
over ice, melting

me till I'm mostly

water. Tomorrow
that dull driving

pain—but tonight
a sweet aftertaste,

bitter before.

*

She was loyal
as a first wife

Beautiful as a second

& rich
as the last—

Or so I thought—

Turns out
I'm the one

More like the widows
who fill my office

With their shady business—

Handkerchiefs doused,
looking for inheritance

Or innocence,
whatever we've lost

& want back—

Always
wearing this black.

*

In bed I toss, half-
dressed, like a wrestler

barnstorming small towns—

Outside, the Black Maria
loud like a barker

rounding em up by the wagon.

*

These days I am the shill
in the crowd, a ringer

Who gets a good one in—
may even win—

Only later there's no one

To split the gate with.
Instead, there's just this

Mermaid, who said
before she cut out

Like a circus
she'd be back around—

Since then
my eyes slugs

Or fountain
pennies, wishing

Under water.

*

She was shiny
costume jewelry

& me a wad
of bills that's mostly

all tish,
or Michigan—

hands around water,
what some call Great.

*

Scratch that. Wet
behind the ears, as paint,

I wasn't. I had no excuse—
knew soon

As she said *I loves you*
that there was nothing

I could do.
Sometimes you gotta let

It rain, forget
you might melt—

Walk all night, drinking
whatever falls

& trying to confess
to whoever'll listen—

Then arrive, drenched, at the station
or saloon or St. Someone, bowing

To the long ovation of rain.

FEMME FATALE

I make men
get religion when

I strut by—
Lordy, they say,

My my—
their eyes are mine

to meet, or not. I turn
mouths to water

& whines
I walk all over—

When I pass by

I'm like a preacher—
though my gown's tighter—

I make folks holler.

I sway like a river
& women grab hold

their husbands' arms
like Jesus', or an oar

to somewhere else
in a hurry. Don't you worry—

no moss grows
on me, this tree

knows which way's free—

Can I help it if I make
men want to run way

with me? Missy,
that plantation you run's

got nothin but cotton—

Me, I raise silk
stockings, blood pressure, lower

flowered drawers—

With me all night it's *Sugar,*
baby, more

And when morning comes
I'll shoo you out the door.   {75}

Said all night long
I'll holler *Sugar*

& more, but when morning comes
Git on out the door.

When I walk by the women
get religion, pray

I'll go away, & stay.

In my six-alarm
dress, in these merciless

heels, I reach
& inch that much

closer to heaven.

THE GAME

Here the ashtrays smoke
by themselves, wind

kicking up enough
thick grey to choke

the dead awake.
I sit with my back

to the wall, face
the glassless door.

This place. Trust
only those you don't

know. When Johnny
Two-Tone waltzes by

silently pat your
packed side. Heat.

Saturday-night
special. .38. The small

door in the back,
a Judas eye, hides

rooms where hands pray
to dice lopsided

as my walk. Flush. Three
ladies. Two ace.

While Abyssinia Ned
cashes in

& Walter Walleye
wins again—a straight—

while Cootie Le Curfew
curses his fate & Delilah

Redbone charms the place,
let's you & me wash

down the day
—a toast—

To my enemies' enemies!

Let's try to spirit away
her beautiful, half-lit face

raising dirty mason jars
of soured grapes.

{77}

THE DIRECTOR

called me in
& on the carpet, let

me know I'd outlived
my usefulness. *What*

was I ever
good for?

I wondered aloud.

Before he dismissed me,
had his two bruisers

—or was it four,
who can remember—

usher me gently
through the ever-replaced

plate glass
of the lobby,

he answered: *Laughs.*

✳

took me out
to dinner, which felt

like the cleaners.
I'd barely dirtied

my napkin with
red-sauced fingerprints

when he canned me,
said my contract

was up & one now is out
on my head.

This week's chippie
picked salad

from her teeth
& swigged the establishment's

cheapest champagne—
like me she

thought she'd always eat
this well, that luxury meant

not wanting
but need. I swipe

{79}

some silverware
& leave.

＊

told me I had a face
for radio & I, for once,

agreed. Said, You know
how you can tell

if co-stars
will click? Place

them side by side, facing
you, & if they make

one set of lips
they'll work. You're in luck,

he smiled, I'll shoot you

at twilight, you'll shine—
you'll get the best

dying lines.

Thank you for your time,
I said, which now

I know was also mine
& was short

as a leading man
who on a hidden platform stands.

*

crowed, You'll never make it
in this business—

You're through—

while a ratty, pampered
lap dog's hind legs

shined his shoe.
He'd taught me how

to fall, to cry
on cue, & now

that's all I do.

On my own, alone,
I headed down

to cover the waterfront
where men drown like sorrow—

at least here the rats
have tails & leave you

before the ship goes down,
not wait till you are sunken

& bone & call those
small ships

built inside bottles, home.

　＊

begged me back
like a balding man

to the mirror & what's left
of his hair. Said

he'd give me the moon,
or at least a room

with a view, top
like my billing—

& by the way all the bills
he'd foot.

I knew he'd never meet
my terms: to swim

with worms, to forever fish
for compliments like food—

So I finished
my desserts, just

enough, & ordered up
another lobster—to go—

then left him red
& steaming

& like the rest of us,
alone—

after telling him that word
he'd never

before heard: *No.*

THE HACK

He lived on cigarettes, burnt
ends & his looks

which weren't much to start—
now had faded like a photograph

in the sun. Vain, head bald
& flat as a tire,

he knew more
than he could say, knew

right before the rain
& was always prepared—after

all, the rag he wrote for was good
only as an umbrella

or the funnies. Dawn
could find him trawling

bars like sand, in alleys fishing
for spent shells

from rifles, holding them up
to his ear as if he could hear

their watery truth. He could
have been in

the comic strips hisself
with his daily falls

& face filled
with spots—close up

he came apart, a flick
without the dark.

*

All his words
were cross. 13 Down:

His favorite, rhymes
with *pluck*.

*

Hack, huckster, he came to
me begging for a scoop—

to tell all & spill. I will,
but not for him, or bills—

off the record I'll reveal
how that private

eye's hands only hurt
themselves, held

me tender till I couldn't tell

whose pulse was whose.
I love that fool down

to the hole, like a knot
or eye, in his shoe—

he, who begged me blue
to stay, or go

quietly, quick, before he got
used, or used

to me. Guess I held on
to him too long like a king

I should have discarded
a while back, given

what else was in my hands,
his wrong suit.

       ✳

Correction: I gave him
everything—grief

& love he didn't deserve.
My eyes long

opened like the dead, I could loan
out enough mess about that man

to keep the presses rolling—

but I'd rather hold tight to my dirt
like a grave. In the end

that hack, slinger
of ink, didn't care

if he wasted time covering
the morgue or the movies

for his scandal sheet—
was the thought of being in either

that kept his hands trembling
& stained by tar

as if awaiting feathers.

THREE

LOW NOON

*

What I like about you is you're rock bottom.
I wouldn't expect you to understand this,
but it's a great comfort for a girl to know
she could not possibly sink any lower.
—THE BIG STEAL

WOW!

Redbone mourns her on-screen life,
her lover and Boss—sometime the same—
who dominate her days and even her sleep,
or lack thereof. Stranded in Shadowtown,
she begins to long for home.

At the bar, or in the car, our man Jones is
missing him some Miss Redbone. He feels
rooked; she took him for his money, and
more. Would more winnings win her back?
Looking to score, he pulls The Heist,
which, like all heists, goes awry. Only thing
that holds him now is jail, pending bail.

Escape might mean her help, sprung like
the season, while he spills his origin to
whoever'll listen. Which is to say, no one.
Cut—

SCREEN TEST

I have given that man,
  like some landlord, most

everything I got—waiting
  now for him

to come & fix my heater,
  to make sure my water

boils hot. Believe
  it won't. Tired,

Lord, of cold
  pouring on my hands

& back, of crossing
  my *t*'s even

when I talk. Round here
  each day is a test

for the screen—blank
  & white, my voice

scratchy as a record,
  wobbling

or too often silent—
  Just sit there

& stay still so
  we can see you.

Yes. That's it—

All day I walk
  round with this face—

at night even my eyelashes
    flutter off. My clothes

I shed like skin,
    or an onion

whose layers line the floor—

& when he drops in,
    which is rare

as the steak he likes
    almost breathing, he'll wear

a grin & his holster,
    his gun a dark weight

pressing my pillow down.

Still, the whole place shimmies
    like a subway

when he holds me.

My only blush
    what I brush on myself—

My beauty marks a map
    to the stars

—swans & butlered gardens,
    the hazel pools & lawns—

which, each night, with enough
    elbow grease & alcohol,

smudge right off.

THE BUST

Lately loving her
is some semi-

annual event—
6 MONTHS NO INTEREST.

Lately, I'm a prefab house,
the kind everyone knows

their way around blind.

Lately, all those hours
I spent holding my breath—

in the shower, or hunched
in a wardrobe trying

not to cough,
after her honey

or hubby or boss
had come home early

& almost caught us—
seem worthless.

Left me only
with a mouthful

of mothballs, pawing
fake mink. Hanging.

In my arms our castaway
underclothes still embraced.

But that's it—
no more kisses, just

waiting while they did
& hoping he'd fall

asleep from her tonic
right quick.

Thank heaven for ledges
or I'd be dead—

too many times I've fled
the back door or

narrow bathroom window
four stories up. Like fire

I've escaped, left
the drapes blowing behind me

like a superhero's cape
freed from under his clothes—

*I needed me
some fresh air,* she'll excuse

to her man, who'll shrug
the window closed

& never know.

STILLS

She put on her face
& headed over to my place.

✳

Cold-cocked
by dawn, clocked awake.

✳

Around me always
signs of a struggle.

✳

This sick no milk
can shake.

✳

The bathroom door said LADIES
but they let her in anyways.

✳

She gets made up & dressed
like a dead man

✳

under the mortician's hand, this
awkward gentleness.

✳

She made her bed,
now everyone lies in it.

NIGHT CAP

He loves me slow
as gin, then's out

light-switch quick.
The moon's burned-

out bulb in a blackened sky,
I lie in the dark & want

his name to be mine—
or to be alone—

Wish I could walk out
this overheated railroad flat

& everyone on the street
knew me, home, & he'd wake

in bed alone & wonder
where I'd gone. Instead,

his unsteady snore—
calling the hogs, sawing.

Sleep, for now, is almost
enough—want it to start

in my toes & tingle
upward, then explode

behind my eyes, closed—
Said start down in my toes

& explode behind
eyes now closed

like the pawnshop
across the street, its sign

blaring all night what
only daylight

can buy. Up
& down the block

you can hear the dogs talk—

never us—till the pigeons
pace the ledge

outside my bedroom & strut
like the painted girls down

on Twilight Avenue,
moan the morning blue.

THE DEAL

She sends me flush
as a fever, or a down-

&-dirty dealer—
I see her

& raise plenty.

＊

Held her close
to my chest, then lost

her like money—

Watch me
ride on vapors & faith

＊

on the way out of town—
no bread to my name—

till I break down.
Follow the crumbs

& I'm home.
I fold.

＊

Nothing's ever
been handed me—she

saves her worst
for me, last, her best

for everyone else.
What a mess.

*

Her hands mean
winter to me—

outside freezing,
warm as sin

within.

*

Once she gave me
a monogrammed kerchief

with a *?*
where my initials

should be.

*

If you want me look
under the tongue

of the city
or in the phone book

under *Yellow*—

*

In my house the best towels
are stolen

from the worst hotels.
In my house the books

are all hollowed out

*

& filled with firearms —
or bookmarked

by small bills. Never
enough. I keep pulling encyclopedias

off the shelf, hoping one will open
a door to somewhere else —

*

a compartment so secret
even I forgot.

THE TAKE

Pockets stuffed with C-notes

like a saxophone
—or Satchmo's horn—

I hit the street sunny
side up. Hair & elbows

greased, strolling, I manage
to avoid her

like rain, sticking
to the eaves—easy

enough to strut & smile
at the world I'm passing by

now that the dice
have rolled for once,

twice, my way—I want
to head into the dark, hit

the first hothouse I see
—drinks on me—

& order up
a double shot of sweat

with a hemlock back.
To your health.

＊

Course, I'd trade all this
for one measley kiss—

would swap my bankroll
for a black-cat bone

if it'd ease her back
like luck.

Barkeep says
I've had enough

& to give my stash
to a dead man to hold

so I can't blow it

like a saxophone
begging her back home.

                *

See, whenever I see her
that girl burns a hole

in my pocket faster
than you can say *Maybe,*

leaves it
no longer swole—

Might as well
head on back

to New Orleans, buy me
the first mojo I see—

Said hitch a ride
down to New Orleans

& kiss the first
hoodoo woman I see—

Maybe some of that there
Follow Me Powder

will reel her on back to me.

*

Without her, my eyes
grow weak

Without her, I'm telling you,
my eyes all leak

& if you see
that stranger sleep

tell him he owes me.
Big.

*

Till then I'll live
on what the dice give—

tapping my foot in time to
my mouth's far-off music—

this blues being
picked up by my fillings.

THE RAKE

Maybe it was the baby
face he carried

round like a calling
card, but older ladies

loved the cad,
thought his shinola

didn't stink. Casanova,
Lothario, Don

Juan de Pollo,
he got widows

to buy
whatever he said,

& him what all
he wanted—

No, I couldn't—

If you insist—

and how.
His sweatless brow.

                *

Slick, the playboy's pomade
made the girls curl

their toes.
Even some boys . . .

For him marriage
was a sacrament best honored

by being put to the test.
More wine

with your dress?
Once he even passed

as a sheik, dark
as he was—

that's how good
his talk—

left a gaggle
of manicured fingers

fumbling in the night beside
sacked-out husbands

to quietly dial The Embassy—
SHadowtown5-4903—

which meant his rented room.
He's never home.

＊

This cat used up
most his nine—

what got him
in the end wasn't the bottle

or a bullet—
though many a shot just missed

his ears, feathering
his hatband

as he slid
the back stair & ducked

out the maid's entrance

after caught kissing the missus
& making the maid

a maiden no more—
No, what

did him in was time,

that jealous son
of a gun.

*

On him the years didn't so much
creep up

as jump—
Cut to him

with skin like linen
& no iron. His nose blooming

carnation red.
He went from vain

to in vain—even
his conk had conked

out, his head's alley filled
with only a few stray

hairs. Homemade
remedies. Here

he is asking for change
like advice—

I give him whatever's left
weighing my purse

& remember that even

tomcats can be treed,
that even hound dogs

may lose the scent
& can't no more fox

or run free.
Are best envied,

not believed—

THE GAMBLE

Night knows me
by name. She like Las

Vegas, the light

From a city nestled
in a desert, distant, toward

Which I been driving—
Oasis she is

The thirst that allows
me to see

Days of dunes shimmering
of sipped canteen—

The funny papers all call
her peril

Her apparel full of heels

Pumps mules
which work me more

Than the old man's farm—
On her I would

Wager the whole caboodle,
sidle up to a green felt

Table and ante
my kitty, lay down

My get-out-of-town monies—

Joe Moore in my pocket
Shortie by my side

A sure thing, a streak
winning—

Like dice we kiss—

She calls me *Gorgeous*
Her r's rolling: *Lover,*

fever, chiarascuro, forever

While she rolls me
for my dough, slips

Me the mickey
the gooba dust—then

Out the back. Sick
broke dumb

As luck, I drive holding on
to the ache of after

Her monogrammed unmentionables

Her laughter
like a track, fast—

Days shot for night

In this garish light
I drive to conjure her

Four Thieves Vinegar
John the Conqueror

Root in my breast pocket—

The scenery that winds past
a screen

I only pretend to see—

She went and put
some kind of hog on me

Only her and hurryment
on my mind—

On its own
the steering wheel turns

Taking blind the curves

THE SUIT

His fingers such a bad hand
of five-card

draw: trade
em all in & still

nothing. Same
crumby pair.

Thinking it was the wind
I let him, knocking, in

with a *shush* so's he wouldn't wake
the bruiser sleeping it off

in the other room. Half
of me hoped

to be caught, fought
over for once.
          No dice—

just that caller, no one's
gentleman, soaked

by rain or baptism

or bathtub gin—he sat
there in the dark that

dingied the room,
night a suit

of clothes, or cards,
he never quite fit.

Begged me like a bookie
for a second chance—

or least his money back.

Well bitten, his hands shook
in anticipation, thinking

this time at rummy he'll win—
discarding, declaring *Gin*.

Forgive me, then,
for reaching out

in the matchbook twilight—

strike here, close
cover before—

to better see him, to warm
his hands with mine & twine

together fingers one more time
before he went out

the way he came,
pockets still flat, all

bets off.
       Like drink,
there's never enough,

he thinks, of me around
in this dry

blue-law town.
In the growing light

I watched him like a house

on fire—helpless
to stop—going up

the hill,
        he walked slow
as a man shouldering ice

he's cut himself
to sell, careful,

before it melts.

THE HEIST

Some tripped silent alarm

I empty round
after round as if at the bar

Hands trembling
like a suspension bridge

This bank heist gone
bad as a marriage.

Radio requesting backup

Me sweating bullets,
endless rounds

Outside, a sandwich board
hawking God

Shotgun smuggled
past security in a flower box

Black mask I can't see
squat out of.

Lady, let's slow drag
as the sirens sound closer

Well-paid police dog
on my tail—

Soon we'll be tropic, taking
baths in getaway green

Letting our skin ripen
& sweeten

The nights crisp
as a banknote Ben Franklin—

Put your hands
where we can see em

Hear the hounds
grow nearer, growl

Outside, the getaway car
leaking gas, tires shot

The megaphone hollering halt

My stethoscope cold
against the vault's locked heart

THE INTERROGATION

The bulb nude
above me, glares

Hanging by a wire

Don't get any
bright idears—

Hourly they beat me
I keep time by

My head's pounding
Cuckoo—

My ticker tired

The pendulum swings forth
& back: good cop, bad

Whatever they want
I will write

Sign here, and here
by the X—

By now my face fits
the detective's 14-karat

Ersatz class ring
For him I will sing

Her praises
My alleged innocence

Above me the bulb bursts
open like a crocus

CASTING CALL

His purported alligator shoes

scuffed, seemed
more like snake to me—

Yay-tall
& tempting, he stood

out among the thugs,
from the line-up

he stepped—wore
the spotlight like a scent.

Yup, Sarge, believe
he's the one—

sorry son
of a gun—I bailed him

to take my arm,
me away.

You sure? my girlfriends
wonder, sucking their teeth

loud like a constable's whistle.

No warning's
no good—

Sometime I need me

some embezzle,
a cockeyed smile

& dangerous drawl.
Silent as a movie,

that man, sometimes mine, hides
his heart in his breast

pocket, longside his flask—
the smallest nip

burns & makes
me brave.

My fingers unringed

His kisses' faint
gunmetal taste.

STILLS

Me
was her favorite charity.

*

She lied like the best;
a white wedding dress.

*

Scars I wear
like a boutonniere.

*

She saved her old stockings
for robbery masks & do-rags.

*

She collected more rings
than a redwood

*

& broke engagements
like records, saying *I'm afraid*

*

You must've misunderstood.
You must've misunderstood.

*

Tonight her every *Dear John* sings;
thanks, trusty box-top decoder ring.

THE ROOKIE

It's difficult being
the guy who goes first

into a room to make sure
the suspect's unarmed—

to test the gunman's aim—

I've eaten like blame my share
of possum

filled with buckshot.

I don't wear a badge
on my chest

but an X.
Easier that way

for anyone to fire back
in the early black—

Once, before the flask,
faith was my bulletproof vest—

Bible in my breast
pocket, its bullet bookmark.

I been grazed
more'n lamb . . .

Soon I hope
to be put out to pasture

& not my misery—
sent behind

a desk instead
of this beat, loud

like a heart, unsteady, always
about to do me in.

＊

How I wanted
home that first year

on the force—
forced to latrine duty,

to *Sir* & meter-maid
on some sarge's whim.

Instead of pats
I got bull's-eyes

on my back.

Still sleep once
made of me mercy

& nights welcomed me
like a distant cousin

not the faithless lover
the dark's become—morning

then meant promise,
promotion, a rising up

the ranks.

＊

Marksman,
a marked man,

I came up with a plan—

not to skim
like milk the way everyone

else did, pillaging
The Widows

& Orphans Fund—
or officers shaking down

simpy suspects
for bail, donations

to ensure a freedom
never realized, nor real.

＊

Lieutenant of the lost,
I thought

maybe if I solved
what couldn't be—

if I opened cases
like cages, like safes

no one else could crack

that'd put me in thick
as thieves with The Chief—

I dreamt headlines
getting my name wrong

instead of this ricochet song.

I fool believed
my off-the-clock footwork

would buy me a trench coat
instead of these turn-

coats who ended up
ending everything—

Never knew
you'd find me

haunting the want ads—
though first give

the obits a glance.

*

First body I seen
wasn't hers

or even mine (I kept
no mirrors, having none

being the vanity
of the young) but a man

whose unweeping wife
found him stepping out

& got her a quickie
divorce with a kitchen knife.

She got half, alright.

The coroner snapped
photos seconds before

the tabloids swooped in
& I could already see

inch-high headlines
would be his only epitaph—

that mine might not
even get written—

& that the dead's only witness
was his dry-eyed mistress.

                    *

Decided then I'd rather
be the private eye

who tailed their affair
& showed the wife

who'd hired him
the black & whites

developed under scarlet light—

Better that than being
the poor missus wondering

waiting with her low light on—

Or than the stiff who now
stares nothing

starring in his own murder
mystery—

Figure I'd rather be
anything but me.

*

Not so
fast. I had

had it, enough,
with the jail that seemed

to taunt me, barely
keeping me out

& crooks rarely in.

I had begged to be let
from behind the desk

but The Chief gave me this
bloody beat

playing mop-up
to graveyard love.

{125}

That was that.
I walked. Left

my badge on Sarge's desk,
picked up my paltry check

& never went back.

*

I hit the bricks
searching for a place

a lease a sign—
for somewhere that needed

only scrubbing, wiping
the soap off the window

so I could see, among the neon
& noise, my name backwards

on the door. That's how
I hoofed my way here—

in borrowed shoes—
only my feet felt new.

THE SAYINGS

Home is wherever
the bed is, the head-

board I banged
my head against—

sometimes with her,
mostly alone.

＊

Today's duds—

what looked clean
at noon—

are tonight's pyjamas

rumpled from an hour's
sleep on someone's floor

& tomorrow's rags.

She wears me out, too—
I need me a new

set of knees
I been begging so long.

A confession: I'm beginning

to like the taste
of drinks dripping

down my face.
These days

she's doused me
enough I've started to pray

the glass stays half empty.

*

Heaven's a small town
slowly dying out

*

Hell's crowded, an apartment
filled with folks who want

something better.
Fire

trucks trapped
in traffic,

backed up because
someone's stopped

to watch. Stubborn neon.
Hell's open

all night & dawn's
an afterthought.

Is too bright. Is sun
reaching down

between tall buildings,
streets stuffed with weeds

like shadow
on an unshaved face.

Scratching. Even when
your number hits

it's never enough . . .

*

Tough. Purgatory
just means living

one place, longing
another.

*

Home is where the hoods look
for you first

but you're never in—
it's where

you can't return
till the coast's clear.

In a word, never.

THE GRIFT

On his back
he lugged around his life

stuffed into a croaker sack
full as a thought balloon

in some cartoon.

*

  Flimflam man, seven
  dollars & a plan.

*

His face looked
like a pool table, deep

pockets for eye sockets,
faded red—but felt

was something he never did.

*

  Flimflam man, ten
  fingers & a plan.

*

His real home was six feet
beneath ground, he was just

up here renting breath
with the rest of us, short-term lease

he's fallen behind on.

*

  Flimflam man,
  two empty hands.

FOUR

ALIBI SALOON

*

*No more harp sessions for me; I am going to hell
and hear some good jazz.*

—BOB KAUFMAN

*This episode starts with a suckerpunch,
and an escape, plus a beltless bout between
guilt and Miss Redbone. Like usual, no
one wins. Just the money-men, who want
our detective dead. Or least bled for a bit of
green. It's getting hard to tell the crooks
from the authorities.*

*Where is she? He frequents his favorite bar,
The Alibi, blending with the scenery and
hoping not to be seen. Unless it's by she.
Will his Hideout be found out? Will he?
For once it's he who leaves.*

*Later, at The Ball, our couple has one last
dance before she returns to the party and
they part. Indecipherable desires: he a
detective of them, she all suspect.
Shave and a haircut, two bits.*

THE SUCKER

I want to be chewed
like the pencil she used

to dial the cops with—
that would be enough—

*

My Method-
acted disbelief

as the pinkertons storm
the building, flooding

the rickety stairs
while I can only stare—

*

Sometimes all
you can do is fall—

Watch the end send
word your way—

*

Give me a gold-
plated hearse

then melt it down
for parts. There's art

to surrender, to staying
in with just a lowly pair

or holding up the teller
with your index finger—

*

Bowing one's head
at the altar

before slaughter

*

To watching it all
wash away

like the cheap dye
blacking the preacher's hair

in the downpour
Or her dusk mascara

& tattletale tears
that turn on

*

& off more
than the water does

around here, bills
past due—

Open up—
how nicely they knock—

me long overdue, too.

*

Might as well finish
sipping my drink

while the pinks
break down the door

*

I'll save my lemon
in case I need a twist

like a mystery
or to make myself

invisible as ink—

*

Bouncing like a check
out the back

*

Unpicked, my pockets
full of passports

each with another name

Only my mien
stays the same

{137}

*

When the bills came
at least I knew

someone still cared

*

Even if it's just
to collect a debt

Or curse
me like she does,

often & accurately—

*

To turn me in

To give the authorities
my sketchy description

*

What a thrill—

while my escape
rope unravels—

to know my name
still spills

her sucker-stained tongue

THE ESCAPE

My car, that dinosaur,
runs on memories

& other things older
than the fossil fuels I tell

the gas jockey to fill er
up with. I toss him

a few bits for his time
& hope he won't recognize me

& call the authorities—
whosoever they may be.

Before the dust
from my bald treads

settles, before he can wipe
the grease from his hands,

my skinny dime's ringing up
the solicitous sheriff

who rallies the posse.

My front-page face
lines every jailbird

& stool pigeon's cage.

I look dead
for my age—

or bout to be
if my shadow

ever catches up to me.

If they nab me I hope
like a catfish my whiskers

will spur their hands, turn
them numb

& like resignation I'll
give them the slip, swimming

into the dark, away.

More likely I'll end up
on someone's table

fileted & splayed.

Son, when you're drug
from the drink

they recognize you
by your tattoos—

I have none so I'll look
like everyone—

after all, a while,

we all smile
like a skull.

THE SNITCH

His favorite word was *uncle*.

＊

Weasely, he had teeth
that floated in his face

like corn in a rusty can.
For a price

he'd open up
his head & spill—

was always in need
of a hideout, but knew

that no house
was safe—that way,

you see, he was far ahead
of the rest of us

who still believed tomorrow
the sun would again stumble

out of bed after another
bender it couldn't remember—

that someone wouldn't
turn us in

because we called them friend.

＊

He knew fingerprints
find their way

on everything, then
wash away red. His lips

sealed, & that seal broken

as a record. Keeps
repeating things. Can't hold

a tune, or his tongue—
he's a journeyman jukebox—

drop a dime
down his throat

& he'll sing. Give him
a hard stare & he'll start

his only prayer: *Deus
ex machina.*

Tonight what I need's a
favor: Tell me

where that man of mine
hides, who he really is

behind his tough disguise . . .

The snitch just smiled,
his palm starting to itch.

*

Soon as I paid I knew
I'd been made—a fool—

To him I might as well
have been the moon—

something distant to discover
& claim, sold

like the bridges
he owns in every city—

Believe you me,
for a song he'll sign

all his deeds
over to you completely.

                *

He was like the world's
greatest lover: would tell you whatever

you needed to hear,
then leave you

wanting more. He milked me
for all I know—

palm crossed,
he sold me snow—

I watched the crowd
swallow him like a sideshow

swallower of swords—
it seemed impossible

yet enviable, what skill
it must take to make

danger your only dinner,
every supper

your last.

THE HIDEOUT

Woke up dead

tired, in my arms
an empty

an instead. Tried
sleeping it off,

my hangover of her,
wishing for some hair

of the dog—or slow purr—

The light my eye hurts

My tongue
white, eyes red.

I am in chalk, an outline,
a back-alley body—

afraid this face
in the mirror (that hides

my strychnine mouthwash)
may be the only one left.

Do I need again

to lose my skin, start
a new town, man?

Grow a beard,
or become one?

I'm sick of taking

it on the chin, of waking
gimlet-eyed from the gin—

Shoe soles like carpet,
or excuses, grown thin.

Cloudy tap water.
One dusty aspirin.

Outside my newsprint
curtains—the black

& white of words,
yellowing—

What I can no more weather

I watch till I'm sure
no light remains

Night staining the streets clean

THE SIRENS

You can hear them hollering
half the night.
    Keeping
folks awake,
me company.
      Hear them
racing to help the hurt

& wonder why not me—
or see them knocking

down doors like death,
under arrest.
     The moon
the bottom of some bottle

night will never drain.
That won't stop

me from trying.
      Night spilling

over everything, thick
as an oil slick.
     Love
the loneliest thing

I ever knowed.
In my head a freight

headed south. In my mind
the mice have quit running,

stopped spinning
their squeaky wheels.

There oughta
be a law.

Outside, that noise
that means need—

what no one round here
seems to get out

         the way for
anymore.

THE MCGUFFIN

She was born yesterday

& in a barn.
Her nails long

as knitting needles,
they clacked whenever

she typed up a report

which was rare
& measured

not by the minute but
the misprint:

Redbone comma
Deliar.

Anyone could see
that secretary had it in

for me—that he
was the reason she set early

her alarm, dropped
like hints pens

& pounds. *You rang?*
her perfume sang.

For a sharpshooter
that flatfoot sure couldn't

catch a clue.

*

You couldn't fool me

with the wool
she pulled over

her sighs. Behind the horns
of her glasses

Behind her beehive
& *honeys*

I felt her sting—

What only alcohol
could heal.

Her thick
black frames like a film

that swam by too fast
to tell it moved—

the water we all tread—

still couldn't hide her
buzzing over him

& eyeing me red.

She played
soft to get.

She may've been blurry,
a bit smudged

around the edges
but all she really needed

was an airbrush,
some patience,

& my best advice:

*Life is mostly
good lighting.*

*

With him
on my arm she had something

to break & sharpen
lead over

Some office door
to throw open without

bothering to knock. *I hope
I'm interrupting . . .*

So when I ran
into her alone—with that detective

on the lam
after stealing a mint—

Miss McGuffin was crestfallen

& all
dolled up.

She'd ditched her prescription

for shadows shuttering
her eyes

propped open
by cocktail umbrellas

& in the fortified-wine light
of the watering hole

was fending off guys

& her tears—
which told me she'd given up

not on him or
on outpacing me—

but on herself.

She'd given in
to beauty.

Case clothed.
The difficulty of staying

put & ugly
was too much even for her

padded shoulders to bear.

＊

High-hatted,

bested at
my own game,

I walked out
the Mirage Lounge

without a word—

she'd hidden them all
in her steno pads

stuffed with shorthand

& ransom notes
& her imagined stationery

as *Mrs. Jones*

that now, for the life
of him, he'd never see.

THE ALIBI

Searchlights gander
the city, I was convinced

looking for me. Convict
of nothing, believer

in the unsteady maps
of stars—I watched red-

nose regulars steam
themselves alive, downing

boilermakers by the bucket.

I tossed em back
myself like smallish fish

or dead soldiers—sent
out to sea, lit—lining

the corner table,
my usual.

Bartender opened me
like a church key

& I spilled everything—

her hair, her silent
offscreen kisses, all

but her real name

which everyone already knew
by number. Her legs long

like a gossip
column. Early

edition. The lobster shift.
Here at The Alibi

it's always late, and whenever
the phone rings

no one's in. It never

rings for me . . .
I see now that thinking

Joe over there's a regular
meant I was one too—that behind

the bar was a mirror
for a reason, not just

to make sure
it wadn't hunting season.

I'm tired of the city
telling me what it needs

isn't me—that mist is more
necessary to the picture

than I am. Pay
the man. Head outside

where the dark gathers round

fires built in the empty
barrel of the moon, men holding

their palms to its light
as if warmth. One hand

flint, the other
a stone—tonight I'll wander home

to sleep a few
hundred years & hope

her poison kiss might
slay me at last awake.

THE KILLER

Born on a showboat
headed upriver, he thought

the world a gamble
& the moon a gin-

soaked ice cube,
whole month

of melting. He looked a lot
like money, just not

much of it—thread-
bare, worn down

by use—stamped
by numbers & years,

a library book
long overdue. Heavy fines.

*

You hated to find
yourself beneath

his oil-slick eyes—

the sweats would start
to overtake you

& you'd hitch a ride

on the potty train.
All aboard.

*

Wearing a splint
like a pinky ring,

he used a toothpick
like a cigarette—

collected guns
& grenades, their rings

long since yanked to take
someone's hand

like a bride.
Once he's been paid

you can't hide—
he'll find you & like

a jukebox fed a fistful
of change, plays his hits

without stopping,
maybe only to scratch.

*

Crow's feet.

*

Have heard him called
a hundred things—

Sleep Stealer,
Death's Little Helper,

Dr. Dirt,
Mr. Red,

He-who-liketh-blood-
on-the-Outside-

Not-In,
The Professor,

The Bumpman,
St. Peter,

Jim Crow,
John Doe—

just never
late for dinner.

　　　✳

No wonder
when he wandered

into Mojo Mike's—where I
was drinking whisky with a little

hot tea tossed in
to honey my throat—I thought

I was done. I skipped out

of there like a steak
done rare, wanting

no more blood
to spill from my side—

headed to the head
to hide.

　　　✳

　　Widow's peak.

*

This is it,
I thought. So

long. Sayonara,
see ya,

no more, farewell,
friends, it's been swell—

ciao, air kiss,
adios amighost—

from now on my *nom
de plume*

is Toast.
Hereafter, hello.

*

Raven-haired.

*

He sat on down
& ordered—who knew

he ate at all, or liked the way
the food here was hot enough

to scar the roof
of your mouth & they let you

alone. The waitress could sense
whether you needed a menu

or carried one in your head
besides a to-do list:

Breathe, breathe,
patty melt, extra cheese.

Vinegar greens.

Through the bathroom door
that never quite closed,

while my stomach, half-
boiled, took a stab

at taps,
I watched him throw back

short ribs & anti-freeze,
drown his insides,

tip well & leave.

*

From the bathroom, trying
not to breathe,

I thanked my stars
& knew if he had found me

like money
nothing could have saved me—

no gin, nor amen.

STILLS

My head hard
as liquor. As luck.

*

Her legs without ash.
Her assets, including cash,

*

kept me going, grey,
& crazy.

*

Bartender, four more fingers
to pour down my throat.

*

My mouth open for her
like a wallet. Her billfold brassiere.

*

Emptied, my tumbler makes it easier
to listen in next door.

*

How she kissed my scars cool—
then left me green,

*

near empty & alone
as a motel pool.

THE WESTERN

Hired guns tracked me down
to the Maybe

Corral, to this two-
horse town, to San Diablo—

streets lined with lead,
dreaming gold—

it filled the men's heads
& bullet belts.

I lined up shots

in the saloon, taking aim
at myself.

These eyes of mine
blank bullet holes.

Posses filled
the streets & even tumbleweeds

seemed after me.
Ten gallons

& chuck wagons.
For once, I was bounty.

*

The saloon's butterfly
doors held

a covered wagon's worth
of silent townsfolk:

miners; majors
in a war

even they can't remember;
the county drunk, lovable

& loud (his family
lost to the epidemic

of '78
we'll eventually find out);

the bald barber;
the mealymouth mayor

& deputy after deputy
who signed up only

to shoot at something.
Might as well mean me.

*

Mostly I stood around like wood,
petrified.

Was dust. Was cactus
comfort.

My slung six-
shooters empty.

In the end I stood ten
paces from everything—

even the cathouse closed

when I knocked
on its revolving door.

My snakeskin boots so old
they've shed themselves thin.

Meet me on Main
at noon

& we'll walk away
from each other like lovers

& maybe,
gun drawn,

I'll turn,
not run.

✳

The gal I came here to save—
who in fact

never asked for saving—
wanders the streets

like the crows do,
wearing widow's clothes—

no more diving décolletage
that drew me to her

first place, once brought me
luck in the poker game.

I pretend
my house is full—

that she's still
like the pistol

at my side, hasn't left me
alone with my back

to the door, black aces
& 8s in my dead man's hand.

She'll mourn no man.

My way
is quicksand. Is a horse

without shoes, & blown plans.

✳

Only this ghost town's
lone store's posters

wanted me

but it was enough
for some bandito to dream

I was reward. Fool's gold—

Dusk surrounding me
like a sheriff

& his deputies whose rusty
stars still shine.

✳

The gunman drew
his Dance dragoon,

cocked at me
like an eye.

I wish him rust.

I wish my trusty
sidewinder

& aim more true
than she'll ever be.

I wish a cavalry
of quiet, not

his off-white hat
& tin star. I wish

him dust
filling his face

& a permanent sunset

while I make my getaway
borrowing his brownish horse

hopped onto from this here
handy porch.

THE CUTS

From me, someone has stolen
sleep—which I had kept hidden

in a drawer under
underwear & my revolver

that I was too broke
to buy bullets for—

why bother.
He is the only

thing that got to me.

*

 My heart for hire
 to the lowest bidder.

*

Love, you see, is something

else you feel
when you ain't

brave enough to hate.
It all goes that way

anyway, so I saves
myself time

by just crossing the line.
Here, all's blur—

life's a nice place
to visit, but I wouldn't want

to die here.

*

I kiss the boys
quick, in order

to get faster
to the cigarette after.

*

I waited weeks for him
to find me again, for his fingers to heal

so he could dial
me up. But the switchboard

musta lost me
like a voice, nothing hoarse

found its way back
to my barn. I've closed that door

only after
he's gone.

*

I like my drinks
& my agents double.

*

Death I know is a place

most folks won't visit
cause they're afraid.

Me, it's cause I know it
too well, like the short lines

on my palm & outside
my door. No one

rings but the collectors,
insurance & rent—

the rest just knock
the door down

to find me, like him, flown.

＊

    I keep around
    a borrowed

    engagement ring
    to cut my way

    out of anything.

＊

Death is a dangerous
neighborhood

you don't want to go
alone—if I ever have to

I carry me
my heat tucked

into my stockings,
snug.

＊

    All my accessories
    are crimes.

＊

When I got there
rope had his house

{169}

surrounded
& the dogs had been called

by some invisible whistle—

There was nothing left
to see—

it was the scene of some time
I could not return to,

though only I
& the crowd

that didn't bother
to gather outside his door

would know.

{170}   ✳

I'm old hat. New shoes
walking away from you.

STILLS

In fishnets her gams caught
any sucker she'd want.

*

The alley fills with bottles & dice
clinking like sidebets, whisky on ice.

*

Choose: heads you
win, tails I lose.

*

At the taboo parlor
the sailor gets inked: *Mother.*

*

She split so quick
I got motion-sick.

*

Dusk finds the sandlot empty
as a cage, outfielders flown away

*

except for the third-hand jacket
warming home plate.

*

My billboard forehead,
her name all over it.

THE BALL

Like a suicide the band was
jumping, hitting high

then low, leaving
nothing but sweat

on the stand. I showed up
to the demimonde masquerade

disguised as myself

& no one recognized me.
My monkey suit still fit

better than I did—
I stuck out sideways

like my bow tie. In knots
over her quitting me,

I had to bogart
this 13th Annual

Bête Noire Ball—

Had some frail
on my arm (part

of my disguise), stars
shooting cross her eyes

from getting an invite—
but inside I was stag,

all solo. My eyes

watched my back
& the front door for

She-who-didn't-need-me

to enter. Incognito,
alleged, I waited

to get close or just
stare her from afar,

but that's, of course, par.

*

On cue she enters,
her eyes 8-balls—dark

& darting & in the end
a prize. Behind them

is where I wanted to be.
At her side hung some guy

far wiser than me,

lipstick smearing
his cheek dark

as a bruise. She glides
the room like a dirigible

& I ain't able
to look away—burns

me up the way that gangster
orders her around

like a drink. Her twirled
pearls. Cloven shoes.

The police, paid off
by pastries, held up the walls

while all over the room
pomade waved like a beauty-pageant

winner right after.

*

I had wanted to save her

like money, then hide
her away, a pearl

under an oyster's tongue.
That night, awkward,

cumberbound, I pretended
to chat like the rest

of the extras—moved uneasy
in the crowd as a mistress

at her man's funeral,
welcomed by no one,

yet known.

*

Among these big fish
& wigs, among lobster bibs

& caviar thingamajigs

I felt like a crawdad
caught out of water, peeled

but quick. Puny me missed
them fish-sandwich women

back home who'd warm
your side & only wanted

some time, a little talk.
Here every painting hides

a million bucks, or none—deeds
locked in a safe—& the ladies'

fingers have enough rocks
to start a garden, a quarry

no chain gang could break.

＊

Even in this
thief's paradise there was little

I wanted: her
smooth hands in mine

dancing slow for a time.
The rest was preface.

After taking a whole roll

of film with my boutonniere,
I had downed enough courage

to cross the room & brush by her
like a pickpocket, stealing

a glance that telegraphed
Meet me in 5.

She did, for old times,
or one last—

As my misplaced date
hovered by the food

& ate with her hands
& eyes, we snuck out

by the pool. I wonder

if it, too, was pulled
by the moon.

*

Around us, frost.

She shivered in her
X-ray dress

so I gave her my jacket,
price tag still in it.

Over time we'd learned
to skip the weather

& *howdy* & the *how-
could-yous*—

To forego the fight entirely

& head, like the heavyweight
finally defeated, to the silence

& bruise & antiseptic
of after. There,

while shadows gathered
in the deep end

I could not swim,

we kissed & my bow tie
turned a whirligig, lifted

me high among the trees
till I could see

how far I'd fall, that between us
air was all

we had left. My eyes oysters

pried open—
shucks.

Her pearlies
a piano I almost forgot

how to play, never got
practice enough.

          *

Didn't want

to let go her hand & sink
back into the blue

but knew I had to. No more

could we disappear
into the dark like a tooth

left in a glass
of cola, or the moon

that, even unseen,
still tugged at us,

sick dentist. Still
we danced awhile

at the lip of the pool, slow
dragging like a cigar

*

till she stole like thunder
back inside

to her life of smiling
when he said to, of betting

against her own chances.
I counted *Mississippi*s

to make sure I didn't follow
too close or brave

lightning twice,
then headed inside

where the party began
breaking things

& up—the drummer taking
down his trap, the bass again

silent, the saxophonist splitting
apart his horn

shaped like a question mark.
We are all

built to be done, remarked
no one.

After confetti, we'll sweep on

home separately
to sleep like enemies:

lightly, dreaming only
of each other's loaded arms.

HEMLOCK LANE

*

Death is a G-man. You may think yourself smart,
But he'll send you to the hot-seat or plug you through the heart;
He may be a slow worker, but in the end
He'll get you for the crime of being born, my friend.

—W. H. AUDEN

After a Midnight Ramble, Delilah walks
home, wishing it Down Home where
moonshine coats the throat. Our private eye
wanders, above ground at last,
looking for her, and his Loot, dusting Clues.
He's close, but only has his cigar.

Finally, The Boss forgives all debts, or meets
his death—and our detective settles for less.
He quits the sauce like he quit the force:
all at once. This, of course, is when
she wanders back in, her atomizer filled
with anticipation.

Will he take her case or the bait? Will she
return to him or home? How special is
her effect? The set is struck, and
the sun sets. Curtains.

MIDNIGHT RAMBLE

Leaving the coffin-cold
theater in winter

Single-barrel moon
aimed above us

He escorted & told me
lies I wanted

To warm my ears

The moon's lazy eye
razored shut

The two of us
fought that hawk

Walking through wind
across a world that once

Seemed so flat I feared
I might could fall off—

Now, Clare, every horizon
got another behind it

Least that's what
Mama would say—*Just you wait*—

But I hightailed it north
& changed my name.

Beneath the shrapnel sky
I wanted to run

From here to the train
& buy me a ticket one way—

I'm tired of eviction
The radio's same station

Playing woe & blues

Said tired of eviction
The radio's same station

Arguing whose man is whose.

I want some diesel bound
south, making all stops—

No more neighbor's
whooping cough

No more leaky
solos from the faucets

Or landlords who pinch,
swapping winks for late rent.

Graveyard-shift moon
that turns men mad—

Let me trade fire
escape for front porch

Let me ride
sunset down to where

Train's the only whistle

& a girl don't got to cry
to keep herself company

Where moonshine ain't just sky
& you can catch catfish

Sure as a man—bearded, polite—
already fixed up & fried.

THE LOOT

I breezed by
the insecurity guard

rode the rickety
elevator—hat off—

to her dead letter office

picked the sherlock
with her hairpin

—luck—then strolled
on in. The scent

of her once-air was
everywhere around.

I drank it down.

No dial tone. Hat racks
& a parasol stand.

I was no bloodhound

just some flatfoot
caught up in the roulette—

the Russian red
of her secretless dress.

I could still see
how her legs stretched,

lounged, all
the way to the ground—

her nails forever
filed like the cabinets

she'd kept in the corner, scrapes
in the wood floor where

any records of us once were.
Her jet-fuel hair.

Preponderance
evidence—the echoing

room emptiness,
her scented wrist—

that muchness I miss.

No one—not even
my sloppy, nicknamed,

overweight sidekick—
had I trusted

till she silhouetted
my doorway, drawled

her slender cigarette.
Smoke rings & underthings.

This morning I woke
in the black—

by noon my books
were blank, figures

red as sunset, as hers—
an hourglass all sand.

Unwound, my pocket watch
stays half-past, or till,

stalled some hour I'll
never undo.

Tonight I sleuth for you

in your new dime store
dye-job disguise, haunting

alleyways & dangerous dives
that own no door for fire.

I always did have an eye
for weather—mercury,

its rough mercy—

I will sleepwalk the docks
weary, creaking,

watching men
lift & load the weight

—the one-way freight
the refused fruit—

onto steamers
that carry stowaways

& hushmoney
slowly, to sea.

THE MOOCH

Like a broke watch he was right
only twice

a day. All other
hours he was busy

borrowing: cash,
your gal,

time. Around him
you better look sharp

or he'd fan you like a movie
harem's eunuch

then end up with your
watch on his wrist,

someone else's fiancée
on his arm.

That momser made
his way through

the world like an ashtray—
full, then

empty, his hands
ashy. He was a Bama,

country, a nobody—

he was a Monday
waking late, no sign

of work anywhere—Fridays
drowned in red-eye,

working the phones—
Sunday spent praying

for so-&-so to return.

By the end so many women
wanted him

dead, it was easier
to count the few

who didn't. Yet
that mook had a hunger

I admire more than smarts
or some fancy-pants pedigree . . .

Adrift on the sea
of the city, excepting

his good looks
& luck, he

coulda been me—

sometimes he even tried
to be, put on my hat

& ugliest face to wander
round the place.

Big mistake: when the goons
found that baby face

they didn't care
if it was fake, or if the name

in his pockets wasn't mine—

just joked you'd think his
alias was *Jesus*

much as he hollered it.
Dead

as that Sea, he
seemed sleeping

when the po-lease
found him—not a cough

or a speech
as in his long dying scene—

stumbling crosstown
bleeding

to his finale—
& me—

his pockets full
of other folks' green,

the fins & sawbucks blossoming—

his shirt stain—
the sirens sounding—

his mouth mouthing blame
& *Tell my mama Sorry*

& *Save me.*

THE TREATMENT

It's always there, you know, the moon—
some rotten hitman

hovering above you—or hidden—
a backlit prop on this back lot

about to fall from
being badly made

like grace. I have grown
tired of running

like a gun, her arms
in their elbow-length gloves

she only takes off
to eat. In this

bidness, love is just
a symptom & death

a side effect. Ain't no cure—

not even her, nor sleep,
neither of which visits

my bed near
enough. In the dark

I keep one ear cocked
like the revolver

in my sweating hands, where
I'd prefer her instead. Rather

hear her lightly
breathe & not be

on the listen for trouble—

who never knocks before entering
& breaking—

counting minutes like sheep
that dance above & bleat

but, like her, never fade
nor stay.

THE CLUES

I had no motive

Lone eye open
I slept waiting for someone

Follow that black car

Where were you the night
of November

Who doctored the documents

The monobrowed thug
The mustachioed mastermind

Over the cliff the cars leapt

A description made fit
my face

I am simply a sketch, an image spit

She a few snapshots, a string
of fake pearl names

For prints I dust her place

THE CHAMP

Tough as luck,
as the steak

at Ruby's Place,

he could put back
half a hog, & that's

just dessert.
Like a divorcée

he wanted half
of everything—the gate,

the diner's menu—

but now he's settled,
like dust, for less.

    *

Not so much washed
as banged up

& hung out to dry

after years of fighting
dirty, or against

what dirt the world had—

Polecat Pete, The Brisket,
Kansas City Steve,

Automatic Slim—
his hands

tarnished & scarred,
he's since swallowed

more pride than blood,
owned by The Boss

who barely let him keep
anything, even his teeth.

*

He earned third
degrees from stone college,

held a diploma from the pokey,

the clink, the slammer—
was sent

up-river after
offing a man

in the ring—
he spent his best

years in the pen,
the can, the hoosegow

till The Boss bought him out

& he graduated
to parole,

the gangster's payroll.

*

Once he'd turned
all comers to beggars.

Once he'd pounded
both black

& white faces
like piano keys

making their moans
a melody.

Once beefy,
bullheaded, now he

was all stock
phrases & stew—

once welter his weight
was now only over,

& watery beer—
only thing left

of his training was forgoing
the ladies. He'd fought

so long his nose had no
more bones

& his ear looked melted
as if made

wholly of wax. The moon
of his mouth

never full again—
he was lucky his teeth,

storebought, still fit.

By night a bouncer
at the Bamboo Lounge

where bright women
from Macon

pretend to hula, shaking
their lovely stomachs

& homemade hair
for dime dancers & stares—

Days he's a bruiser,
a thug, a loser

looming over you
like a building, playing

the Chicago piano,
the tommy-gun violin.

To the gods he gave

good as he'd been dealt.
If only

Daddy hadn't left.
If only

the damn ref
hadn't called it—

he was poised for a comeback

about to get up
off the stained mat.

His ears still ring
with that.

＊

The Boss's left-hand man,

he was now a night school
of wishes swimming

a cloudy aquarium,
a tiger trapped in a rage—

with a mug like that
you'd think he'd have more

brains to fill it.
Head hanging, arms forever

folded like the flag
given to the widow

after a twenty-one-
gun salute. Taps

play when he walks
into a room. Last thing

I wanted was to hear him knocking
the door or my head

off its hinges—knew
that thug wouldn't quit

till my face, & fate,
looked like his.

THE DIVE

Young men here guzzle
& dream of becoming drunks

& regulars, the drunks
here dream of becoming

young. I wait

for her one hour, promise
myself no more, then wait

half hour over.
As I'm pretending

to don my fedora, some hood

arrives to tell me she ain't
coming, never, no matter

& I better quit callin.
Pats his pistol-padded side.

I wish that I was a wish,

that rubbing this bottle—
gin's djinni—would give me

more than mist.
The stooge suggests

I find another date,

to learn a place
where the smoke don't stain you

& the glasses wash up new.
Like fatback

his knuckles crack.

I excuse myself to the head,
looking for an escape hatch—

cursing her name, planning
never to forget her.

She gets under

& infiltrates, she's foreign
intelligence . . .

No dice. Windows sealed
by the past & paint—

Dreaming of a back way

I read some last words
on the wall, faint—

*Don't sleep
With a gangster*

Or his wife. Just don't.

Nor a waitress,
some wise guy retorts.

Then something I don't
remember penning—

Reports of my death are

greatly anticipated—
but it's my hand sure

as shooting.

THE INVASION

They came with ray gun
& strange diction.

They came in peace.

They came for me in masks
made to look

like someone
else I knew well—

They zapped.
Thought themselves

far advanced
in their shiny suits.

(They never did detect
my Lazarus device.)

They spoke
stilt sentences, galactic

silences, a tongue

recognized by no one—
only by my telepathic

interplanetary translat-o-meter
nabbed from the lead scientist.

In wire-powered saucers
they buzzard & hover, sparks

showering like praise
or meteors.

Their every gizmo glows.

Radon, radar, radio-
active, panty raid—

They wanted
our women, p.a.'d

we were in for it. Goners.
Kaput. If only we had the ore

they'd come here for . . .

Their hides' true colors
green as money, as me—

They borrowed like sugar
their neighbor's skin

Blinked slow, like television

Until everyone I knew
was a Martian.

Until, to the tune
of a queasy theremin,

I gave in. Ran.
As for women, you can

have mine, who never was
mine after all—

Eyes dry as ice

Me & the Robot tried
revving up the rocket

crafted from spare parts,
an engine jerrymandered

out of rage
& adamantium—

making our way

to our own heavens.

THE STAND-OFF

Parked my Packard
by the edge of the wood

And waited

Dusk began the deep grass
The groan of gravel road

Made sure I was not
followed

Like a soldier I slept
sitting up

Shamus, private
dick, flatfoot, sleuth—

At the end
of Hemlock Lane, alone

Revolver in my lap
like luxury

The bouquet
of bullets beside me

On edge, I wait

Red-eyed moon
my only mistress

Faithful, fatale—

I've sold my last
soul, stood

Awhile at Crucifix Road
unsealing every deal

All to no avail

Mole, double
agent, spy—

Along the edge
I park, weighted

With night

Found out there's no flunky
no heavy but me

The woods a city
Pines swaying like a subway—

Counting stars like enemies

I wade out
neck-deep in night

Investigator, hoarse voiceover—

Earlier,
in the Underworld Inn

I begged Barkeep to hide
this packet of words in case

They have to drag Midnight Lake

In case I should
disappear, no trace—

My name off
the glass door scraped—

THE PAYBACK

Stripped, de-
briefed,

cowed, found
out, frisked,

confessed, pled,

tired, treed,
left for dead

& for good, forgot—

lurched, lost,
scalded, belted, shook,

rooked, finked, ratted
out & on—

withdrawn, strapped,

harried, pursued, deluded,
deluged—

bit by dogs
hounding my heels—

jilted, jinxed,

downed, fawned
over, ferreted,

sated & abetted, sent

into the lion's
living room—

parlayed, parlor-
tricked, sicced

on, surrendered—
quailed, quitted, shown

the door, the boot, given

the bum's rush,
the lady's luck—

botched, black-
listed, decked, sawed

in half, duped,

dried out, dusted
off, sobered, handed

my hat, running out
of excuses & room—

I came clean.
Forgive me.

As in the dream when you turn
to face them that chase you

up the endless stairs
I spun

& found no one.

Turns out all
that hunted me

was me—haunted
by what I believed

she to be. So I gave up
some green, flashed

a few fins around town,
greased

the underworld's
squeaky wheels

& got let off free. Left
to my own devices—

which are few,
& idiot-proof.

She was permanent yet
faded, a prison

tattoo—I once thought
like that serum

she'd be true

but I know now
I was wrong as a sweater

on a sheepdog.

THE WAGON

My reputation
exceeds me. Temptation

littering the bar, chanteuse
piano-perched, her sifter

of brandy empty. Fifths
of watered whisky.

Wagoned
for a week, I'm no good

to anyone, soft-
boiled, unsalted.

Haunted—
her quinine kisses

her microphone caress.

Wanted to hold her like her
two-faced fur stole,

that foxy smile.
(Instead teethmarks

punctuate my skin
like perforated parentheses.)

Barkeep's glass
eye like an olive

The sharks circling the pool
table in the back, sniffing

out green. Felt
myself losing my arm

wrestle bout between
sarsaparilla

& something stronger.
Sleep.

Step on out
into the cold—under

the awning bouncers
stomp & nod

like hunched horses,
their breath billowing.

Lovers pass in hansom
cabs. Who will stop for me,

screech at my jaywalk, honk
to let me in? The moon

winking its way across sky—
I hail like Mary

The Charon Cab Co.

to sail through the city—
my cabbie, an escapee

from the state, swerves

& swears at the salt-
covered cars

brushing so close
you could lean out

into wind & plant
each one a kiss.

EYEWITNESS

The adders are at me
again—like men their kisses

chill & sweeten
send me asleep. Am plumb

tired of waking next
to the dead—

of going to bed blind

then struck awake
by the sight

& stank of them.
The blue—the bottles

of silence, emptied, about.
The ringing—

am through with running
a bath to scrub

my body, evidence—

my eyes a camera
that can't forget.

No cyclops counting
sheep, looking for the men

hid beneath wool,
worsted—I know sleep only

as powder, or pill,
a strong thing that pulls

me downstairs, my lids
like a coffin's, half-closed.

Fools fall
for me, then tumble

the rest the way,
sixteen stories. Or say

they love me, lying,
& stumble into suicide

surprised almost alive
by the note they never wrote

found scrawled in their own hand.

What I have seen. Have teared
& smeared my handkerchiefs

& remembered to call out
the right name—swept up

any stray hairs to fatten the fire,
my alibi. Tidied,

I place the practiced panicked call

& wait till the cops come
to draw another name in chalk.

Hit the streets shaded—

I cannot stand
to watch the photographers swoop in

like crows—they cluck
& snap

at the corpses lined up—
sudden flash—

before coroners lift
those sheeted bodies

like bellhops with oversized
crocodile bags—toe-tagged,

unclaimed.

THE PAWN

My dancing days
    is over. I will walk

with my legs in hock,
    praying rain—

my hands empty
    as a gun.

I once held her tight till
    I could hear

her heart through
    her padded brassiere

beating soft my ear—

Now sorrow trails me
    home like a lost puppy

that won't protect me
    & I need to feed

& name.
    I'm afraid

it's got me licked.

The heart's a hassle.
    A hustle.

You can try to hide it
    neath your hat

or wrinkled zephyr-
    weight jacket—

still it hammers out
    loud her name.

Faint.

Tomorrow, I'm telling you,
    I'm gonna go on

down to the pawnshop

& buy back my blues
    from the man

I sold em to—
    pay him twice

the dues, the small
    scratch, they fetched

just yesterday,
    when I was flat.

STILLS

I want to play me
in the movie.

＊

Even her thoughts
cost. My penny-free pockets

＊

lined with lint.
Heaven spent.

＊

With me, unfortunately, moxie
is just a drink.

＊

Around each finger
a string as a reminder

＊

of what, I don't remember—
settle bar tab? try to forget her?

＊

My luck so bad she musta had
shoes beneath the bed.

＊

Next time she threatens to split
I'll grab her grip, help her pack.

SOUNDTRACK

Banging out a symphony
in a typewriter key, I didn't hear

My door creak open, only
her *Ah-hum* & perfume

My knocking knees

When, uninvited, she sat
herself down. Crossed

Her legs like the county line

& I, some boot-
legger driven far

For such strong lightning.

She leaned & asked
once more could I find—

A friend? her man?
something so valuable

She could not say?

Anythin,
was once my answer—

Had spent off-meter hours,
hundreds, snooping for her

Working under the cover—

Was left with only
a fake-mustache rash

& some prop glasses
without glass.

My heart twin
cufflinks then.

＊

Tonight, her eyes welling
over like an oil rig,

I let my mind, like
a housewife, or eye, wander:

August again
    & I eleven, filled with Sunday

& early supper—
    hummocked, happy.

How the sycamores sang,
    the cicadas.

This is long before
    gunfire, before the Colt

& rope & a river
    I am still swimming.

Long before I arrived
    our starved city, before derringer days

& nights even darker for all
    the streetlights . . .

Her hands tapped
an impatient Morse, fanned

Two lace gloves. *Well?*
Her veil smile.

Adam's-apple bob. Ceiling-fan swirl.

*

I thanked her for
her time, then sent her

Away packing, teetering
on unsheathed stilletos.

Her kisses tender, a resignation—

I may be back
to her like an undertaker

Whose scent no one can shake—

For now I'll ignore the lack
of knocking, the quiet

Except for wind
& tin-roof rain,

The phone's pleading ring.

{223}

THE TITHE

Darkness edges out dusk
by a nose & night's

just another wager

I've lost: for once
I thought the day

wouldn't end. Instead,
lay me down like a bet

in the almost dark
& dream: rain

you can drink,

Mama young again,
my palm

like a tree, shake it
& out drops money . . .

Wake with the cold

& my arms halfway
round my own shoulders—

no help.
Like drunks the streetlights

sing me awake
while down the street

at the storefront church
I swear

they're calling my name—

warning the men to behave,
the women

not to be like me, to beware
& not let me near

their front door. I am Sunday's
hum, or holler,

Saturday's last damp dollar
left at the altar.

FAREWELL

Her tears fell
like apples

Like Paradise the tears
fell, like Rome

My eyes now
are open, and ready

for business
A stand of concessions

Like the Alamo her
tears fell, fighting

To be remembered

There's a quiet
in this room that cannot

Be caught by film
Such a scene—

Like crocodiles her tears

Like the *Fin*
ending a foreign flick

Walking away, back
to the camera

—It's that quick—

No assistants
to assistants, no key grip—

My eyes a double feature

Tears falling like a cliff-
hanger heroine

Like horses
in a nickelodeon western—

Awkward and
final, tripped

By unseen wire

THE END

Me, tired as time is
of forward, of the smallest

things—the tidying.
My office a hurricane.

She breezes in

with those red eyes
& quiet—my climate

out of control—
sudden cold.

Her dress backless

My baited breath.
Hold all

my calls.
My fresh-spackled walls,

poorly patched bulletholes.
Cigar smoke

catching my throat.

After a fruitless frisking,
I ask, *Miss,*

what can I do you for?
An hour

or more. Tears mascaraed,
enough to fill two hundred

inkwells. The hard sell.
I fill

my arms with her bills
then pour us each a double

shot of deals. We all
know how it'll go—she will

stay awhile, flashing that smile

as if tomorrow's front page
won't tell all—her newlywed

name—her photo
found guilty—or me

headlined *patsy,* found
face down

breathing water.
Finito. For now,

roll the fake rain—
cue the moon

& track my slow-motion

walk through town
yelling *Cut.* Fold up

these cardboard storefronts,
dismantle the days

& deep-six the streets—
all are slated to be replaced

by Roman ruins, a teen beach,
or beardy, biblical plagues.

CREDITS

The city at last let me
leave it—streetlights

just on—no sunset—
the scent

of laundry rising up
from beneath a grate,

starched by hands
unseen—Mama's,

I imagine. I have had
it all, enough

of water cold & clogged—

have a mind, half,
to walk these weedy blocks

to the station where a midnight

train tugged me
nine months back. I step

careful, avoiding the cracks.

Everywhere,
late-summer hum—

no crickets, just the smack
& holler of children playing

stickball—no
mound, no sliding,

no nothing but beans
& pork, asphalt & fence, far

as I can see. Stoop talk.

You can keep your cans,
kick em all day—

I can taste already
Mama's tomatoes coming up

from the earth like a mummy
—slow, heavy, hungry—

in the B movie I always
end up in, playing

Screaming Girl, Secretary,
or Victim #2. I always did feel

sorry for that man wrapped up
in his past, made awake

by grave robbers as if newlywed
neighbors. *How d'you do?*

The name's Clarice—
though down home everyone knows

to call me Reece & not
to bother phoning, just

drop on by. The train lurches
the station—all points south—

till I am a star like all the others
in sky—winking, flashing strings

of pearls like citified words—
flickering like the Luckies

I will hide, buried
with pride & *told you so*s

beneath our unscreened porch.

FIN

END TITLES

[ONE] HONEYMOON RAIN

VOICEOVER *(reel one)*   3
The Set-Up   5
The Chase   7
Speakeasy   9
The Hunch   12
The Chanteuse   14
The Props   16
Dress Code   18
Premiere   22
Rendezvous   24
The Hush   26
Stills ("With her, guilty")   28
The Ingenue   29
Stills ("When we met")   32
The Office   33
The Subplot   37
The Alias   39
The Suspects   41

[TWO] STONE ANGELS

VOICEOVER *(reel two)*   47
The Boss   49
The Races   52
The Ruse   54
The Gunsel   57
The Rushes   60

Early Show	63
Stills ("We undress shy")	66
Saturday Matinee	67
The Frame	69
The Hooch	71
Femme Fatale	74
The Game	76
The Director	78
The Hack	83

[THREE] LOW NOON

VOICEOVER *(reel three)*	89
Screen Test	91
The Bust	93
Stills ("She put on her face")	95
Night Cap	96
The Deal	98
The Take	101
The Rake	104
The Gamble	108
The Suit	111
The Heist	114
The Interrogation	116
Casting Call	117
Stills ("Me")	119
The Rookie	120
The Sayings	127
The Grift	130

[FOUR] ALIBI SALOON

VOICEOVER *(reel four)*   133
The Sucker   135
The Escape   139
The Snitch   141
The Hideout   144
The Sirens   146
The McGuffin   148
The Alibi   153
The Killer   156
Stills ("My head hard")   161
The Western   162
The Cuts   167
Stills ("In fishnets")   171
The Ball   172

{239}

[FIVE] HEMLOCK LANE

VOICEOVER *(reel four)*   183
Midnight Ramble   185
The Loot   188
The Mooch   191
The Treatment   194
The Clues   196
The Champ   197
The Dive   202
The Invasion   204
The Stand-Off   207
The Payback   209
The Wagon   212
Eyewitness   215

The Pawn 218

Stills ("I want to play me") 220

Soundtrack 221

The Tithe 224

Farewell 226

The End 228

Credits 231

ACKNOWLEDGMENTS

Thanks to the editors and journals that published the following poems, sometimes in slightly earlier forms:

Callaloo: Speakeasy, The Chanteuse, The Frame, Stills ("In fishnets"), The Game, The Gamble
The Canary: The Alias, The Suspects
Code: Rendezvous
Conjunctions: The Wagon, The Hideout, Midnight Ramble
Fence: The Props
Grand Street: The Set-Up, The Chase
Kenyon Review: The Killer, The Sucker
No: The Boss, The Races
Ploughshares: Stills ("We undress shy"), Stills ("With her, guilty")
Poetry: Early Show
TriQuarterly: The Loot, The Subplot.

Thanks to the Guggenheim Foundation for a fellowship that allowed me to complete this book, and to Indiana University for its continued support. Perpetual thanks to my agent Eileen Cope, to my editor Deb Garrison, and to her assistants Ilana Kurshan and Millicent Bennett.

Special thanks to those bad movies and good friends who, often through an unwitting phrase or a great suggestion, helped these poems along. "The Boss" is for Colson Whitehead, who said the book needed a boss, and who helped me edit this talkie; "The Alias" was supplied by Nicky Dawidoff, and the poem's for him; Cathy Bowman suggested I write a "Femme Fatale" and unknowingly gave me the poem's last line; Jonathan Railey helped find the toast for "The Game" one night in Flicker; Richard Eoin Nash helped me see more clearly the "Stills," which are for him; the poem "The Invasion" was lost on an aircraft until a kind stranger, Lisa Todd, found the notebook it was begun in, and returned it to me; and the title "The Gunsel" was only one thing of many given to me by Kate Tuttle, who gives me so much more each day than she can know, or even this book, which is for her, can repay.

A NOTE ABOUT THE AUTHOR

Kevin Young's first book, *Most Way Home*, was selected for the National Poetry Series and won the Zacharis First Book Award from *Ploughshares*. His second book of poems, *To Repel Ghosts*, a "double album" based on the work of the late artist Jean-Michel Basquiat, was a finalist for the James Laughlin Prize from the Academy of American Poets. His last book, *Jelly Roll*, won the Paterson Poetry Prize, and was a finalist for both the National Book Award and the Los Angeles Times Book Prize. Young's poetry and essays have appeared in *The New Yorker*, *The Paris Review*, *The Kenyon Review*, and *Callaloo*. He is editor of the anthology *Giant Steps: The New Generation of African American Writers*, the Everyman's Library Pocket Poet anthology *Blues Poems*, and Library of America's *John Berryman: Selected Poems*. A former Stegner Fellow in poetry at Stanford University, and recent Guggenheim Foundation Fellow, Young is currently the Ruth Lilly Professor of Poetry at Indiana University.

A NOTE ON THE TYPE

This book was set in a face called Eldorado, so named by its designer, W. A. Dwiggins (1880–1956), as an echo of Spanish adventure in the Western world. The series of experiments that culminated in this type began in 1942; the designer was trying a page more "brunette" than the usual book type. "One wanted a face that should be sturdy, and yet not too mechanical. . . . Another desideratum was that the face should be narrowish, compact, and close fitted, for reasons of economy of materials." The specimen that started Dwiggins on his way was a type design used by the Spanish printer Antonio de Sancha in Madrid about 1774. Eldorado, however, is in no direct way a copy of that letter, though it does reflect the Madrid specimen in the anatomy of its arches, curves, and junctions. Of special interest in the lowercase letters are the stresses of color in the blunt, sturdy serifs subtly counterbalanced by the emphatic weight of some of the terminal curves and finials. The roman capitals are relatively open and are winged with liberal serifs and an occasional festive touch.

COMPOSED BY CREATIVE GRAPHICS,
ALLENTOWN, PENNSYLVANIA

PRINTED AND BOUND BY BERRYVILLE GRAPHICS,
BERRYVILLE, VIRGINIA

DESIGNED BY GABRIELE WILSON